My Books

NON FICTION
How to Live with Bipolar
Bipolar 1 Disorder Rescue Plan
37 Symptoms of Bipolar Depression
The Bipolar Guide
Life Lessons
A Practical Guide to Overcoming Loneliness

FICTION
(Pen name Dorothy Alter)
Shards of Glass Series
Shards of Glass
Fragments of the Past
Memories Lost in Time

SHORT STORIES
One Summer

POETRY
We Never Did Mornings

HUMOR
Funny Old Folk

List (c. Jan 2025)

Copyright © 2025 Sally Alter

All rights reserved. No part of this publication may be reproduced, stored in a retrieval system or transmitted in any form or by any means, electronic, mechanical, photocopying, recording or otherwise without the prior permission of the publisher or in accordance with the provisions of the Copyright, Designs and Patents Act 1988 or under the terms of any license permitting limited copying issued by the Copyright Licensing Agency.

LIFE LESSONS

SALLY ALTER R.N.

Contents

Introduction	9
What is something you learned unexpectedly from living alone?	11
What have you learned about fear the older you've gotten?	15
How can I practice cultivating flow in my life?	19
Can I figure out what life is all about in my 20's?	21
Why do we get that sad, lonely, empty feeling sometimes even if we have had a good life?	27
What should I do to learn how to love myself and accept all my flaws?	31
Do you think depression is a life long illness or can it be cured?	35
Did you realize shortly after getting married that you had made a huge mistake? What did you do about it?	39
What is your best advice on living alone and overcoming the challenges that solitude and freedom can bring?	41
How many 70 year-old women are all alone, and how do they deal with it?	45
What life event made you take drastic measures?	47
I'm worthless and ugly and I don't have anybody or anything. There's nothing left of me but a hollow, broken spirit. What can I do?	51

What is the most amazing thing that happened to you at an airport?	55
Is your life like the one you imagined, or is there an improvement or a disappointment?	57
What do you do when you realize you are alone for the rest of your life?	63
Who was the most disturbed person you knew personally? What did they do to earn this title from you?	67
What is the most absurd question someone has asked you about England?	73
While sorting through a deceased person's possessions what is the most disturbing thing you found?	77
Why don't very old people seem to get bored?	79
How can people tell if you are not confident in yourself?	83
What are some useful things that people learn too late in life or never at all?	87
I hate everything about myself. How do I start loving myself more?	91
I live far away from my family and there is nobody to share my feelings with. I have friends but they aren't interested in my feelings. What should I do?	95
Is 39 considered old? I have so much to accomplish, and I want to travel and enjoy life more, but I feel too old.	99
How can I find happiness if I am unhappy in life?	101
How can you avoid feeling that everything in your life has been insignificant?	105
How does a person heal from childhood trauma?	107

Can you learn to be more spiritual in the same way you learn about facts, or is it more of a heart thing?	109
How did your marriage end?	113
What has your life been like?	119
What is the best way to deal with hatred of someone?	123
How can we help someone who is very depressed? What should we never do?	127
Does life just happen to you?	131
What advice can you give to lonely people?	135
How horrible is depression?	139
When did you stop caring what other people thought about you?	141
How should I reply to "How are you," When I'm not fine at all?	143
Nobody truly understands me, not even my family or friends. I always feel that I'm alone all the time, and I have to face every problem on my own? How can I feel better?	145
What life situation took you a long time to understand?	149
What do I do when I feel like a piece of garbage with no redeeming qualities, and will I die alone because nobody cares enough about me?	153
What happened to you by accident that changed your life for the better?	157
Nobody actually cares about me. What do I do now?	161
What causes some people to be happy alone while others need people around them all the time?	163
About the author	170

Introduction

Welcome to a journey that spans over seven decades, a journey filled with experiences that have shaped not only my life but the wisdom I'm about to share with you. I'm now 76 years old, and as I look back, I see a tapestry woven with threads of joy, sorrow, triumphs, and heartache. This book is my way of offering you a piece of that tapestry – a glimpse into the lessons life has taught me.

What you hold in your hands is not just a book, it's a conversation. It's a space where I respond to the questions that many of us have grappled with in our quietest moments. The answers I offer are not the result of academic study or theoretical ponderings, they are the fruits of a life lived fully, with all its ups and downs.

As you turn these pages, you'll find a reflection of your own struggles, and triumphs. Loneliness, marriage, depression, self-love, spirituality, confidence, happiness, trauma, and the feeling of being misunderstood – these are just some of the themes we'll explore together. Each answer is a response to the complex, sometimes overwhelming, questions that life presents us with. My hope is that in these words, you'll find the wisdom, comfort, and inspiration you need to face your own challenges with renewed strength and clarity.

This book doesn't belong to any particular genre because life itself defies categorization. Life is too rich, too varied to be boxed into one label, and so is the advice I offer here. Whether you're seeking practical guidance, spiritual insight, or simply a new perspective, I invite you to delve into this collection of thoughts, reflections, and answers.

In sharing my experiences and lessons, my greatest desire is to connect with you – whoever you are, wherever you are in life. I hope that by the time you close this book, you'll feel as though we've had a meaningful conversation, one that leaves you with a sense of clarity, purpose, and most importantly, hope.

So, let's begin this journey together. Bring your questions, your doubts, your hopes, and your fears. I'll do my best to offer you the answers you seek, drawn from the well of a life well-lived. And perhaps, along the way, you'll discover that the wisdom you're searching for has been within you all along.

What is something you learned unexpectedly from living alone?

When my husband died suddenly, by suicide, I was left totally alone with no family at all in this country, no money, and only his credit card debts. He took his own life the day I came out of a mental hospital after a month's stay for bipolar disorder. During my 18-year marriage he wormed his way into controlling every aspect of our daily lives. In the end he was the one who decided if I should buy lipstick, or walk the dog, and I didn't even have a key to my own house.

When we first met in London in the late '80s, I was a successful Marketing Manager of an American hospital group. I had the Southwest Region of England, a company car, a generous expense account, and good salary. I also owned my own car and my own house and had paid off the mortgage.

But, when somebody is controlling, their methodology is to pluck a person's life away from them hair by hair. At first it is jealousy, then come the accusations of unfaithfulness. Then it's keeping the person away from friends and family; isolating them from society. There is the editing of the person's emails, the timing of their phone calls, then the limiting of spending money, and finally the captivity of that person in the house. I can't believe it now, when I look back, but I was even locked in my own house when he went out and told not to use the phone or he would find out.

After 18 years of this kind of treatment, there wasn't much left of the old Sally. I felt like a cipher and of no consequence to anybody. I felt worthless, hopeless and lost.

After he died, the first five years I spent in a dreadful rage that just would not stop. I was unable to work because I was so ill, went back to hospital another six times, had to relearn how to drive, even relearn how to write a check. And had absolutely no idea about paying all the bills which immediately rolled into my empty hands. I had to be taken to the bank and shown how to open an account. I couldn't stop shaking.

Now to answer your question.

What is something I learned unexpectedly about living alone:

Well, I have learned that I can be self-sufficient, smart with the finances, make new friends, socialize, and even enjoy my own company.

Since his death, I have gradually gained my confidence, and am now able to enter a store without having a panic attack.

And more than that, I have realized that I am creative and have written nine books to date over the past three years.

So, living alone is now a blessing. And there is nothing like having full control of the TV remote and the thermostat.

What have you learned about fear the older you've gotten?

Well, I am in my seventies, so have had a lot of time to experience life. I have learned that human beings experience a mixed bag of emotions every day, but if I think very carefully, I would have to say the most prevalent emotion people have is fear.

This may seem overblown because it is true that many people do not seem to be afraid of anything. They would certainly never admit to being afraid of anything anyway. Yet, none the less, I think it is fair to say that we all experience fear to one degree or another.

The average person lives with many fears every day. They are afraid they will never meet Ms. or Mr. Right. They fear they will miss meeting their soul mate altogether. They are afraid they will fail in their work, or their schooling. They are afraid their kids will turn out badly. They are afraid they, or someone they love, will get sick and die.

Death is the biggest fear of all among humans. It is something we would rather not think about. But death is a fact of life. We shall all die someday whether we are ready to die or not. You could say death is just another part of life and we had better get used to the idea. But death brings more fears with it than anything else.

How will I die? Will I suffer? Will I be alone or have the people I love around me? These are all valid points, but most of them are beyond our control. Of course, the lucky few (if you can call them lucky) are those who die in their sleep. For some reason these people, the lucky ones, have it much easier than the rest of us mere mortals. They just go to bed one night and don't wake up the next morning? The rest of us are left to cope with the loss.

Then there are those who are so afraid of their demise that they fail to live. Their fear is so great that they dare not even leave the house. It is not as if there is anything definite they can pinpoint as a real threat, but it can seem to those people everything "out there" is a potential threat to their safety. Even, or especially in some cases, the weather. This is when fear becomes a disorder we call anxiety.

We are all left to wonder, one way or another, what will happen after we die. People who have faith do not have the same fears as others because they have been brought up to believe they will go to a better place called Heaven when they die.

But on a dark night, when everybody else is sleeping, the thought suddenly pops into our minds that we are totally alone in this world. We may have a big family, be part of a large community, but the fact remains that we are alone, whether we like it or not.

Some people have a Dark Night of the Soul where they experience existential angst. They wonder what life is all about? Why am I here? What is my purpose? Why do I exist? And sadly, the longer we live, the more likely we are to look back with regret, thinking of all the opportunities we missed in life along the way.

This poignant realization of being totally alone in the universe is frightening beyond anything else. That is where our real fear lies. Yet there is no knowing what is out there waiting for us. We don't know where and when time ends. On a cloudless night, we look up at the stars and wonder what life is all about.

The only thing we can do is to appear on the stage of life and muddle through the best we can. We are all passing time until we die. And death is the only certainty in life, after all.

How can I practice cultivating flow in my life?

*If you are serious about your endeavor,
you can practice like this:*

Come to realize that 'flow' means there are good and bad events in one's life. Imagine the waves on the sea. If the weather is fine, the waves are just ripples, or the sea is calm with no swell. If the sun is shining on the water, tiny diamonds seem to sparkle on the surface. It is akin to smiling. When diamonds dance on the water this means that life is going particularly well for you.

This is good flow.

However, when storm clouds brew, the waters darken and

send frothy waves leaping many feet into the air. You can even sense the blackened waters churning inside you. Sometimes these waves are very rough indeed and capsize boats. Men drown. This type of sea is not to be reckoned with, but to be respected.

This is a bad flow.

The answer is to 'Go with the flow'.

Floating lazily on the calm sea is bliss. It is a gift and takes no effort whatsoever. When you are experiencing bliss, you are free to share your gift with others of your choosing. This is not the time for anxiety. You need not worry about coming to the end of your bliss because you are prepared.

Appreciate what life has sent you.

Inevitably, the day will come when the storm clouds brew overhead, and the waters will gather and darken your day. They send plumes of spray into the air and will threaten your bliss, but if you are going with the flow, you know you are safe. You will not drown. Let the waves take you where they may. Do not struggle or panic, just realize that bad flow will not last.

Bliss is waiting a few days away.

Can I figure out what life is all about in my 20's?

First of all, no, you cannot figure out what life is all about without having lived it. Simple as that. However, I am amazed that you would come up with such a desire. I never thought about anything beyond being twenty when I was twenty. And beyond being twenty-five when I was twenty-five.

But if I was going to start life again, I think I would have given it more thought because my life has been a mess one way and another. I am not saying I would have planned it as such, as it really is impossible to plan things because change happens all the time, but I might have thought things through more carefully.

I wish I knew more about you but as that is not possible, I shall have to imagine that you are an ordinary person with no particular handicaps to contend with. If you would really like to think ahead, I suppose the best thing would be to imagine what would be really important to you later in life.

As I am in my seventies, I can only look back and marvel at how things have turned out for me. The rise was good, the plateau was great, but the downhill slide that I had to contend with was not what I would have liked or imagined. And I blame poor planning on my account for most of that.

I think it might be useful to you to compartmentalize the basics in life and see how you can make them work better for you. Although my life has turned out completely different from the norm in that I have no family, I am thinking that you have the usual parents, siblings, grandparents, aunts, uncles and that sort of thing. I hope they are supportive.

Most people's lives are really basic. They are born, go to school, go to work, get married, get a mortgage, have kids and grandkids, then they die. Sorry - but that's about the size of it. But how successfully you do all these things is up to you, and it wouldn't hurt to think about each compartment and what you want to get out of it.

For example - if you go to college (or you may already be there), you might want to study things that will be of use to you in your future career/s. As everything is about technology these days, you would be well advised to further your skills in these subjects. There is much more to college than this, of course, and I hope you will have fun while there. Learning is what life is all about, and you can never learn enough.

If you want to travel, you might want to make another compartment for this. Travel takes a lot of money, even if you hitch hike, so putting money aside now would be a good start. I also advise you to take time off when you are young as you may be ill and/or broke later in life and miss out on many adventures.

Money wise, there is never enough. So, when you are young it is a very good idea to get into the habit of saving. I regret not doing this earlier in my life because putting away a couple of hundred dollars every month now amounts to next to nothing. It is a good idea to budget each month, and to pay yourself first – for example put 10% or 20% of your income into something that will grow as the years go by. And don't touch it. If you are able to do this, you will be amazed at how much money you will amass in your lifetime. This will allow you to do just what you want later. Of course, there are many exceptions to the rule, and you need to have fun too. Life without its pleasures is very boring indeed. So don't forget to develop interests, hobbies and groups of friends to enjoy them with.

Marriage and kids, I can't really comment on because I made a mess in both of those departments, but you might like to try to envision the future with whoever you marry. Many people, including me, marry without any idea of their partner's expectations. It is never okay to assume anything in life. Just because you want two children, don't assume that your partner will, too. And if you assume that he will want to share the chores (a big bug bear with me) you may be shocked when he doesn't. You may find that you want to live in the suburbs while he wants to live in town. There has to be a lot of compromise in marriage.

Work. Unlike the 'good old days' when people had one career, and stayed in one job for forty years, people nowadays often have many careers, especially now we are living in the technological age. It is a very good idea to learn all you can when you are young and build on that knowledge all the time. Be flexible. Don't be stuck in the same rut. Enjoy your work. Be happy to make something of your life. It is true that many jobs are boring, and people only work to get their pay at the end of the month, but if you can work at something you are passionate about, life will be much happier.

So, we have covered most of the basics in life. Does it sound boring? I think so, but I wouldn't recommend all my turmoil's to anybody either. We have covered money, work, marriage and kids so the one big thing that I haven't mentioned, and which matters the most in the end, is health. It doesn't matter how much money you have, if you can't get up the stairs because you have wonky knees, or because you have congestive heart failure, you are not likely to enjoy your expensive trip around the globe. I would recommend that any young person finds something they like to do to keep fit. Being strong and flexible in body is the same as being strong and flexible in life.

I hope this doesn't all sound too basic/frightening/boring/challenging - but this is life. Make sure you learn something new every day and do the things that make you happy.

Why do we get that sad, lonely, empty feeling sometimes even if we have had a good life?

Yes, that's a very interesting phenomenon, isn't it? It is perfectly true that we can be living an okay life yet be empty, sad, and lonely on occasion. It is quite unnerving. It is an emotion that arises from within us. You are quite right about that.

Just when you think everything is going well, up pops a horrible feeling that suddenly overcomes you. Where you once felt content, now in a matter of a blink of an eye, you find yourself sad, empty, and lonely.

It is difficult to say why this happens, except to say that it happens to most people at some time or another. It would seem to be part of the human condition. I tend to think we are not destined to be happy all the time. Happiness is overrated. We can be happy some of the time, then totally miserable in a matter of minutes.

I often wonder if this is because we are all alone in the world no matter who we are married to or who we have in our lives. We are totally alone in our heads, and nobody can tell what we are thinking. Conversely, we cannot tell what other people are thinking either. We move from one thing to the next in order to be happy.

I have to say, I think life, with all its chaos, is merely a distraction from what is really going on inside. Life, you could say, is a smokescreen which blocks what we are really feeling inside. It seems we need that smoke screen, and all that racing around trying to be happy, if we are to survive in this life.

What is behind the smoke screen? That is the question. And a very interesting one it is.

Do you know why you are distracting yourself with other people, work, kids etc.? It is doubtful that you do, unless you have spent a long time thinking about it.

Basically, if we are human, we are always under the threat of death. We have no idea when we will die, if we will die a natural death, or suffer for years. We just don't know. We might wake up one morning and find ourselves worrying about our demise for no particular reason other than we had a bad night's sleep. We suddenly think what would happen to us if we were to die in the night and didn't wake up.

This is such a terrifying thought for most people; they need the chaos in their lives to successfully hide from that thought. Just imagine, you have had a bad night, and you wake up feeling afraid that you could have died in your sleep. What do you do? You quickly leap out of bed, put on the coffee, get your breakfast, kiss the wife, and rush out the door to go to work.

Then, of course, you will be alone at some point in the day. You will need to get to work for a start, and you will certainly spend time alone in the bathroom, if not elsewhere. So, what do you do? You quickly avoid thinking about death by planning what you will do for the rest of the day - phoning a client, checking your emails - anything rather than be alone to think.

We are all the same, just racing through life day by day, avoiding thinking about our demise. It is quite unnerving, so, we do all we can to distract ourselves. We love to keep busy.

I have been particularly interested in loneliness as I have been alone now for more than twenty years since my husband died. I have suffered a lot of loneliness in my time, but now I am used to my own company, and enjoy my solitude.

What should I do to learn how to love myself and accept all my flaws?

Loving yourself is probably the hardest thing you will ever do in this life. Many people go to their graves with hatred in their hearts. It really amazes me, when I think about it, that hating or disliking oneself seems to be the norm in this world, and I think it is very sad indeed.

Why do we all hate ourselves so much?

All I can tell you is that I hated myself for many years, but slowly learned to love myself, and now have no problem being me.

So why this big problem? Why do we get up every morning, do what we have to do, look in the mirror and hate who we see staring back at us?

I have to go back to childhood because I believe that is where all seeds are sown. Everybody has a different experience of childhood; some are better than others. But there is no doubt that what we learn when we are small lives with us for many years.

*We even convince ourselves that this
is who we really are.*

However, I have discovered I am no longer that wilting pot plant that sprung from that lowly seed. Somehow or other, I have passed that stage for ever.

So, what is the secret? If you think about what I have said, you will realize that in order for a tiny seed to grow into a beautiful plant it needs nurturing.

Love

It needs a nice place to grow, for a start. If that tiny seed should be thrown into infertile soil it will have a hard time getting its bearings. Many of us know that feeling, to be mixed in with the clay and rubble, and trodden into the dirt, even before we have had the time to grow roots.

That is very sad indeed.

Now, it is becoming obvious, at least to me, that the tiny seed that is you needs a nice place to grow. A secure place that feels comfortable out of the wind and the storms. If this can be achieved, we are halfway there to loving ourselves.

That little seed needs a place to survive and thrive and that is exactly what many people need to learn. There is more depression caused by our immediate surroundings than anything else, yet many people have not come to this realization, thinking that alcohol, cigarettes, drugs and sex are the answer - they are just smoke screens hiding what is the real problem. They are an expression of self-hatred.

What does the "good" mother do to nurture her baby? I have never been a mother myself but have been witness to many mothers who have doted on their children, given them what it takes to make a child grow up happy and healthy. It seems to me that the love of a "good" mother is all that little seed needs to thrive.

So whatever it takes - just love yourself like the "good" mother would do. Give yourself all the love that a tiny seed needs to grow straight and beautiful. Plant it in fertile ground, water it every day, feed it when it is hungry, even talk to it when you are on your own.

Your plant may not be as beautiful as you would like. It may have torn leaves or even disease, but it still needs your love.

Perhaps more so, who knows?

Soon enough, you will be able to look in that mirror and see your true self. The one you love.

Do you think depression is a life long illness or can it be cured?

Since I have had bipolar disorder all my life, I have had more than my fair share of depression. Because of that experience, I am able to empathize with people who are suffering in the same way. And I have written many answers on Quora about how it feels, and what to do to recover.

Seeing as I have actually recovered many times, I do not think of it as a life-long illness, although with bipolar disorder you never know what is around the corner. Some people with clinical depression have a very hard time with recovery, and some remain in a depressed state for weeks or months. But it really is not a death sentence because it can be overcome. I am resisting using the word "cured" because that suggests that it will never recur. That is not always a given with this disorder.

However, since writing on Quora, I have evolved through many different methods of coping with this devastating illness. I have suggested medication, therapy, tips and tricks on what to do, relaxing into it, but I am now beginning to look at depression in a completely different way. And I will be sure to practice this if/when I am next depressed.

New thinking:

Looking at the world as a materialistic place, it is becoming clear to me that the materialistic world has little to do with depression.

I am seeing depression now as cut off from all this, maybe in an amorphous world of its own, away from all the humdrum everyday tedium - get out of bed, take a shower, eat your breakfast, do what you can for the rest of the day. All this "doing" is exhausting.

It is beginning to seem more like a withdrawal to me, a delving down into the spirit, grasping at the root of our being. You could call it a retreat if you like, a place where monks go to get away from this materialism which is our world.

So, with this new thought (and I am thinking as I write), it seems to me that a depressed person should turn to spirit for help. By this I mean dismissing the outside world and delving down into what really is

The Self.

This can be achieved by cutting oneself off from the rest of society, taking cover in bed if necessary, lying in the darkness with nothing but one's own thoughts however gloomy they may be. The absence of light, sound and the hustle-bustle of everyday life would make this inner world more poignant and easier to grasp.

When in this little, dark world of yours, it is easy to liken it to the womb. Here we are curled up in the fetal position, listening only to the mother's heartbeat, and gradually emptying the mind of all thought.

In this position I think it would be very possible to be reborn - to slowly, very slowly emerge into the light and be kind to oneself. After all, kindness is akin to spirit in all its forms. Do whatever you think your mind and body requires to get well. You will know this by instinct.

I don't think this is the complete answer, of course, I have a lot more thinking to do on the subject of depression, but I do think it would be worth a try. There is nothing to lose.

Did you realize shortly after getting married that you had made a huge mistake? What did you do about it?

I was only 19 when I was first married. He was 20. The wedding was fine, but the moment we walked into our rented apartment, my new husband said, "Into the kitchen, woman, where you belong." Accompanied by a shove.

Things degenerated rapidly after that. I remember locking myself in the bathroom for hours in order to get away from him and being made a fool of many times in front of our friends, and his family.

Unfortunately, I was very young and had no family or anywhere to go, so I just sucked it up for eighteen months.

We (or rather I, because it was half of my inheritance) bought a house about sixty miles away from London, but the marriage was just a farce at that stage, and I suffered a lot of physical and sexual abuse.

Anyway, I decided to move out and found another flat to move into. I arranged my things in the cupboards on the right side and piled his stuff on the left. I then instructed the removal men to take the furniture and leave everything that was on the left side on the floor. It was quite a scene, and my mother-in-law who lived next door came running out of her house screaming and shouting, and chased after the removal van.

I never looked back.

What is your best advice on living alone and overcoming the challenges that solitude and freedom can bring?

I have lived on my own for 23 years since my husband died of suicide.

Twenty years is a very long time to be alone, and I have no family in this country, either. Yet, here I am alive and well, and really enjoying life as never before.

I am trying to think back now to see if I can answer your question truthfully.

The fact is that some people have no option but to live alone. Life is sometimes like that. Things happen and we are forced into a situation we don't necessarily want. Whether we go kicking and screaming, or relaxed and happy depends on a lot of different things.

In my case, I was very ill after my husband died and really could have done with somebody to help me. Many people said, "How could you live in this house when your husband killed himself in here?" Well, that may sound like a reasonable question, but when the answer is, "I have no choice," it makes people realize that sometimes there is no choice in what we experience.

I have to admit to you the first few years were very hard. I suffered a great deal of loneliness, and it was demoralizing. However, you eventually get used to your own company and can see many advantages to it.

I found a great therapist after my husband's death and am still with him today. He is responsible for keeping me alive as staying alive was not something I wanted to do. As I say, I was very ill and there were many other reasons why I thought of ending my life which would not necessarily apply to other people. However, I didn't succumb to that temptation and simply learned to adapt. If we don't adapt, we go into extinction like so many animals on the planet.

The way out of my dire situation was not through socializing and making new friends. It may be nice to do that, but it didn't work for me. I tried various churches and groups of people who were interested in the same things as me, but when you are alone everybody seems to be in couples, and you are rarely invited to join them.

Learning to be alone and content is a process. It is really a process of learning to love oneself.

This can take a very long time, or it may not happen at all. It all depends on how much effort you are willing to put into changing your lifestyle, and way of thinking.

I changed my lifestyle by accepting that I was alone and not trying to do all the things that I used to take for granted when I was part of a couple. I did not yearn for somebody to talk to, nor did I want to go out and meet other people. I simply realized that I could be happy on my own and could even enjoy my own company.

As for loving myself, that did take a long time. Going from hate to love can seem insurmountable, but it certainly can be done because I am quite happy being me these days and am enjoying my solitude.

What has eased my loneliness is that I got two cats early on and they have been a lifeline. Sadly, both of these cats have passed on, but I now have other cats to keep me company.

I also found that distractions are really important if you want to be happy with your own company. I have many hobbies and interests so can lose myself in those for many hours, sometimes even forgetting to eat or drink.

My life is not the same as your life, though, so what you do will be different from what I do. Overall, I would say the thing that will save you is acceptance.

It is sometimes hard to accept things you don't want, but I can assure you that it can be done. Once you have accepted your situation you will be free to love being by yourself.

How many 70 year-old women are all alone, and how do they deal with it?

I am in my 70s - unbelievably - and live on my own. In fact, I have lived on my own for the past twenty years. Due to the fact that I have no family, I live on my own in America. I am from London so am far away from home.

This may sound rather bleak to you, but it is just like anything else. You get used to it.

I enjoy my own company and keep myself occupied all the time. During the daytime I write books, write on Quora, read, paint or watch TV. In the evenings I read, watch Netflix or You Tube videos.

It is not an exciting life, but I am not miserable.

I also have bipolar disorder and manage to take care of myself. I am what they call 'high functioning' so can live alone with no help from anybody.

Everything is fine except when I need people to do things I cannot do. Once my microwave oven blew up and I knew I couldn't carry it out of the house, nor could I carry in a new one. However, there is an activity center in town that helps with this kind of dilemma, so the Volunteer Coordinator dropped in after work and took my microwave away with him. He came back the next week to install the new one I ordered from Amazon.

If a person is resourceful, there are usually ways of managing the hard stuff.

The only time I miss another person is when I just want to chat to someone. Nothing in particular, just comment on everyday things. Then I would like somebody here, but not under any other circumstance.

If I could hire a chatty person for an hour or two a week, I would. Other than that, I manage quite happily on my own.

What life event made you take drastic measures?

You could say I have had a very eventful life, and you would not be wrong. There have been so many life-changing events over the past 60 years or so that it is really difficult to find one that stands out from the rest. However, I shall start way back to when my mother died of asthma, and I was only fifteen and still at school in London. My father had already died of a sudden cerebral hemorrhage when I was ten. But, for now I shall write about what happened as a result of my mother's death.

My little world really did collapse at fifteen, and I literally had nowhere to go. My widowed mother took in 'lodgers' for a few years. We had a lady of ninety-two, Mrs. Burns, in the front room downstairs for a while, until one day she came running into the kitchen, shouting at my mother, "You are a very wicked woman, you've stolen my money." Of course, my mother hadn't touched her money, but being a very patient woman, she said nothing, then reached over and pulled out a long string from the front of Mrs. Burn's dress. There, dangling in the air, was the little silk purse where this sweet, little lady stashed her worldly wealth between her breasts. I came home from school one day and found her room empty.

We had two law students in the front room over the garage, Rosemary and Judy. They were both young and very giggly. Seeing as I was still a little girl to them, we didn't have much to say to each other. However, we also had an Engineer who only stayed Monday through Friday because he went home to his family in the country at the weekends. We got on great. He built me a pair of stilts and I hardly got off them, even in the house.

Then when my mother died, my younger brother Bob and his wife Susan sat everybody down in the lounge and told the lodgers they had to find other digs. Judy must have been really upset because she couldn't stop crying. The house was put up for sale, all the contents were haggled over by Bob and my sister Marion, (I was the baby of the family) and I was suddenly looking for a place to live. I had another brother, Peter, in Australia. He was called immediately to see if he could have me over there, but as he pointed out I had no money to get there, and besides they had no place for me to sleep. My sister Marion, who took most of the stuff in my house, couldn't possibly have me because they were so squashed into their basement flat as it was that my two nieces had to share a bedroom. So, Bob and Susan, who had no children, seemed to be the only choice I had left. My sister-in-law Susan, who was not known for discretion or empathy, made it very clear she didn't want me living with them because they had no more room than Marion. Also, I had a little poodle puppy. A very nasty scene ensued, and I ended up having to take Susie back to the breeders.

So, I moved in with my bike, a small bookcase, and a bedside lamp. Everything but my clothes were sold or gone. I had to sleep on the couch in the dining room and put my clothes in the sideboard. Sleeping in the dining room was a problem, though, because when their friends came to dinner I was in the way. So, I was told to stay out of the house until late in the evening on those occasions.

We did have some happy times because I liked to cook with Susan, and we both liked to dance. I have fond memories of the two of us listening to Chubby Checker on the radio and doing 'The Twist.' But many fights ensued over my being with them, until one day Bob got a phone call from Susan who told him she was waiting in a phone box until he decided who was to go, her or me. You know the rest of that story. So, when I was in bed that night my brother came into my room, sat on my bed and told me that I had to leave, and he would call my brother Peter to send some money for my fare to Australia in the morning.

I didn't wait around. I got up and went outside in the middle of the night in my pajamas, walked to my boyfriend's house and asked him to take me to my sister's house in London. I can see this is going to be a very long story so I shall end it there and leave the rest to your imagination. That was my life-changing event before the age of sixteen.

I'm worthless and ugly and I don't have anybody or anything. There's nothing left of me but a hollow, broken spirit. What can I do?

I can easily see myself in you. I had your mindset for many years. I too thought I was worthless and ugly. I had nobody and nothing and certainly could never find love.

I wrote reams of poetry about being hollow and broken. I dwelt on that misery for the best part of my life. I painted a whole glut of gloomy paintings to prove my point – but who to?

Myself.

When you have had a background of negativity, and ugly things have been said to you over and over again, it is so easy to start to believe them yourself. You think that if the people who told you those things really meant it, then it must be the truth.

I was not broken after all.

The fact is that if you feel hollow inside, it is your responsibility to fill that vacuum with loving thoughts. It is up to you to fix it.

I also learned that relying on other people for my happiness was a mistake. People are far too busy with their own misery to have the time to worry about yours.

Slowly, I began to like myself.

This was such a new concept for me. I found it hard to imagine that I was a worthy individual. But, I dared to look in the mirror and discovered that I was not ugly at all. This had been a misconception.

And most of all, I began to realize that I was not worthless either. That was somebody else's opinion, too.

That realization was dynamite. Thinking you are worthless destroys your confidence. It makes you feel ashamed to be you.

So, I began to take a leap from liking myself to loving myself, which was something I had never dreamed of before.

Loving oneself does not come easily, especially for people like you and me who have been led to believe that we have absolutely nothing going for us at all.

I used to cringe and get mad when the TV commercial for L'Oreal hair products came on. Every time I heard the words, "Because you are worth it," I was so incensed that I had to mute the sound.

Now, here I am, able to watch that commercial with no problem at all. Now that I realize that love comes from within and not from somebody else's opinion of you, I have gradually filled up that hollow space inside and feel that I am worth it, like everybody else.

I have junked the poetry and the pictures of that shell of a person. I can no longer recognize myself in them. I am a worthwhile person.

I love myself.

It's funny how I can now look in that same mirror and see beauty and life. I now see a whole person who is loved and comforted, and no longer broken.

You too can grow that seed in the dark chasms of your mind. Become that late-blooming flower that you are destined to be.

What is the most amazing thing that happened to you at an airport?

Fifteen years ago, when I went to visit my brother in Australia, I had one of the worst episodes of Bipolar Depression I can ever remember; abruptly changing time zones like that is a common trigger for people with mood disorders. Just trying to get the medications right on the flight is a big challenge because the morning medications soon become the night medications as you cross the time zones.

The flight path is from San Antonio, Texas to Los Angeles on the west coast of America, then on to Sydney, Australia where I had to change again to get to Ballina where my brother lives. As soon as I got there I sunk into a major depressive episode, and my energy level plummeted to zero. My brother had organized a full itinerary of all the things he wanted me to do, but I was so ill all I wanted to do was sleep. I just remember being dragged from here to there in a kind of zombie state, unable to appreciate anything.

By the time I was due to come home, my mood had degenerated even further, and I found myself in a total fog not knowing up from down. He drove me to Ballina airport and put me on a flight to Sydney. When we arrived in Sydney, a couple of hours later, I was totally disorientated. I walked up to a flight attendant and asked her which flight was going to San Antonio?

She looked very puzzled. "Do you mean San Antonio, Texas?"

"Yes," I said.

"You're not in America yet," she said. "You're still in Australia".

I don't know if that is sad or funny, but it certainly didn't make me laugh.

Is your life like the one you imagined, or is there an improvement or a disappointment?

I was hoping nobody would ever ask that question because I would be compelled to answer it.

Let's see. When I was young, I never really imagined that my life would amount to anything at all because I couldn't see past the next couple of years. As you know, young people think 21 is old.

I certainly didn't expect to be an orphan by the time I was 15, searching for the rest of my life for a mother to replace the one I had lost. In fact, I married three men thinking that I would be accepted by their mothers. I never was.

There was an unspoken expectation in my family that, if you were a girl, you would be a good wife and mother. I failed at both. There was never a thought given to education, career or anything that took brains. Everybody presumed that I had none.

I found out that people went to university when I was 19. Nobody in my family had ever been to university, and nobody really thought about it. I finally went to university when I was 56 because my therapist wanted me to prove to myself that I wasn't stupid.

It really did a lot for my self-confidence and proved that I wasn't as stupid as I thought I was.

I never imagined that I would get bipolar disorder when I was 15, and spend the rest of my life swinging from one crazy mood to the next - taking a multitude of little colored pills, doing mood charts, attending peer group meetings, going to a clinic for 28 years, even having so many hospital stays that I spent 14 months of my life behind bars in various mental hospitals.

I never imagined I would be married to three men who abused me physically, emotionally and sexually. For a long time, I equated abuse with love. I never got that one right, and now find that I have been living alone for the past 23 years since my late husband's suicide.

I never bargained for that either.

Never even thought he might die, even though he was 16 years older than me. And I certainly never imagined, in a month of Sundays, that he would commit suicide and leave me ill and alone in a foreign country.

I have since found out that I really like living on my own.

As for kids? Most people just have kids without thinking they might be unable to do so. They plan their families even before they get married and savor the happy event even though there's not much to look forward to in the future.

I never thought about having kids, I just imagined, naively, that they would appear without planning, or something. But I had an ectopic pregnancy when I was 25, then realized I really did want kids, badly. I spent the next twelve years in total misery; doing ovulation charts, having operations and procedures, and avoiding everybody who was pregnant. I am only now able to look at babies, some 55 years later.

I never appreciated the way they thought it was okay to force me to look at dozens of pictures of their kids, even knowing that I couldn't have any.

Now it's streams of pictures of grandchildren.

When I finally realized that kids were just not going to happen, I gave up and married a man who had had a vasectomy.

Not by design, of course, it just happened that way.

Having been born in London with no thought of living elsewhere, I have been totally shocked that my life has turned out to be one of continuous travel.

I married a man from Malta. I had never heard of Malta, but soon found I was living there and really enjoying it.

Then we moved to Scotland. I had absolutely no idea what to do with my life so, when I walked into a job agency, I ended up becoming a nurse. I had never considered being a nurse. But I did that job quite happily for 11 years.

My second husband loved to travel so I tagged along, of course. Visiting 22 countries and finally living in 4 different countries in the world was certainly not something I imagined would be a normal part of my life.

Later I married a man from New York. I had never given New York, or America for that matter, a second thought. They had never appeared on my radar. But here I was married to a man who wanted to take me to America and travel in an RV around the country. We spent 6 years traveling full-time from State to State, then bought an RV in Amsterdam and traveled around Europe for 6 months, staying in 9 different countries.

At first, I was blissfully happy. But I had never imagined what a control freak he was, or how much it would devastate my life. I soon ended up without a grain of self-confidence and a life in tatters.

Getting past 54, which was the age my mother was when she died, was certainly something I had never imagined. I ever thought I would be a widow at 54 either. But here I am 76 and still kicking.

Saving money was like having kids. I never thought about it. I even gave up my nursing pension to go abroad. And now I find, because I only worked for 19 years in England, I am only eligible for half the British pension.

However, despite everything, I would say that I have made a success of the life I was given. I now love being my best company, living in South Texas (I never imagined I would live in Texas), doing exactly as I please.

I have had immense joy out of doing artwork - oils, acrylics, pastels, watercolor, collage - anything really that has stretched my imagination. I have also written 9 books.

I am sorry this has turned out to be a very long answer, but when you have lived a long life, there's a lot to talk about. I imagine I would have been hard pressed to write more than a couple of paragraphs if I was 21 when answering this question.

What do you do when you realize you are alone for the rest of your life?

I'll tell you what you do -

You realize that being alone does not amount to being lonely.

Being alone is fine, but being lonely is hell.

I have been through both scenarios and have survived to tell the tale.

When I was first alone, way back 20 years ago, I was very lonely. Every day was a nightmare because I had nobody to talk to.

I noticed sharing things like passing the time of day with

someone became very important. Just commenting on mundane things was the stuff of life. I could comment on a new bird at the bird feeder and there was nobody there to say, "Oh, yes, let's look him up in the bird book."

I also noticed that sharing decisions was very important. It soon becomes apparent that there are many decisions to be made in any partnership, and there is nobody there to share disasters when they occur.

When the a/c breaks down in the middle of the summer there is nobody there to share the decision of which company is more reliable to fix the a/c system. You find you have to try them all, and when you are a single woman, it soon becomes apparent that there are many rogues out there who profess to be something they are not.

When you are young and single these things do not matter because people, mainly men, will go out of their way to be helpful, but as you age so does the help available. So, when you are old and single you had better be prepared to feel lonely much of the time. But as human beings, we eventually get used to situations - people can endure the worst of situations and still live quite peacefully.

Over time, sometimes a very long time, your particular situation begins to take on a new light. Rather than feeling the sting of loneliness, you find that you are beginning to enjoy your own company. It is quite a surprise. How could you have ever imagined you would prefer being alone? Yet, that is what has happened to me and I daresay many other lonely single people.

Over time, I have adapted to being alone and plan on being alone for the rest of my life. I look back with amusement because I was a social butterfly when I was young, always surrounded by company, always craving more.

Now, I no longer crave company. In fact, I generally shy away from it.

I notice these days that I am quite content with my writing and my cat, and when my day is interrupted by people, I get bored almost immediately and just want to be alone again.

My friends are few. But I don't mind. If I have a couple of people to talk to every now and then, it is enough for me. I don't need to be texting and talking on the phone for hours like some people do.

My quiet life is just that. Quiet. I get up when I have had enough sleep. I eat a bar of chocolate for dinner if I choose. I jump in my car and go for a drive if the mood takes me, and there is nobody there to complain.

I was married to a big-time complainer for many years. I felt chained like a dog in the yard. My chain wasn't long enough to stay out of the sun, and my bowl of food was always way out of reach.

Now, I have dropped that chain for good, and I can please myself whenever I choose.

Who was the most disturbed person you knew personally? What did they do to earn this title from you?

Three people have earned that title from me. I could write at length about my second mother-in-law because she was choc-a-block full of weird idiosyncrasies. Having long mastered the art of offense, it was nothing for her to tell me, "You really should do something with your hair," or "I sometimes wonder why my son married you,' "or "I can't understand why you don't get a better paying job." Waltzing into a fancy boutique with me in tow one day, I was reduced to a burning, red bubble when she told the manager, in no uncertain terms, that she should get a new buyer for their shoes.

I could also write about my first husband. Being young and impressionable, I found his eccentricities puzzling but quite fascinating. When I first met him, I was drinking illicit lager with friends in a cafe on Richmond hill, and he strode in with his head held high and just sat down next to me. I was shocked, to say the least, because I had never seen him before in my life. He was such a sight that my friends had difficulty stifling their laughter. Like a character in a play, he wore a three-piece, pin-striped suit and a silver fob watch on a chain that he kept in his pocket. He checked this watch continuously while he puffed away on huge cigars, mashing them out in the already overflowing ashtray. Driving home with him was quite an experience, watching him speaking on his telephone in the console of his old Jag. As I say, I was young and this was the 60s, but even so...

My next-door neighbor is a really colorful person, too, with her scarlet hair and her far-too-short shorts in the summer. I have to look the other way when she bends down to weed her flower beds. But she really is something with her on and off attitude, leaving me reeling in amazement time and time again. It's a case of she likes me, she likes me not. She's like the blinking light on a lighthouse. She will speak to me, even wave, for a couple of weeks, then it's back to nose in the air, and "tut, tut" every time she sees me coming. I think I am a friendly person, but she obviously doesn't agree with me.

However, all things being equal, I really have to admit that I am the most disturbed person I know. Of course, you never really know yourself, but judging by my crazy bipolar behavior, I am not sure I want to. When in depression everybody around me is on pretty safe ground because I just sleep, but when in mania I really live up to my tarnished reputation. Quite honestly, there are just so many incidents I could reiterate, it would be difficult to know where to start.

But bear with me. In church one day it was announced that a newly wed couple had lost everything in a fire in their new house. I hardly knew these people, but in my manic state it touched me so much that I rushed up to them, tears streaming down my face, assuring them that they were welcome to stay with me even though I only had one bed!

Or how about the lecture given by a local Professor. My brain and my vision must have been screwed up that day because I just couldn't work out what she was talking about. She put a stone on the floor and talked about how we can only see one side of the stone most of the time, when there's always something going on on the reverse side. This was so weird to me that I detained her afterwards and said, "But how could you see what was on the other side of the stone from where you were standing?" "Err!" Strange look screwed up face, no response. For some reason I didn't realize that she could see all sides of the stone because it was lying on the floor in front of her.

Then how about all the unmentionable psychotic experiences that come hand-in-hand with mania in bipolar 1? The Fire Department, and all the lovely, big, burly firemen are pretty much used to me and call me by my first name. It often seems to me that something is burning in my house, even though it is all electric. I can clearly smell smoke. I pace up and down, sniffing for hours, even crawl into smoldering sheets in disbelief. Then when the firemen arrive, it's always the same old thing. A big hug and "Sally, there's nothing burning in here, but we'll be sure to check it out for you."

There have been so many incidents I am rather stuck for room on Quora, but perhaps the most exciting hallucination I had was when I was driving through a forest with a friend at night. She was in a great mood until I said, "Stop! Stop!" She stopped and couldn't see what she was supposed to look at. "Look at those silver deer leaping out of the trees." Well, I suppose that was a bit over the top, even for her, so she dropped me off and I never heard from her again.

And lately, I don't think I am ill now, but I am doomed to consequences at every turn. Mostly, it is words and phrases, exact words and phrases, even unlikely ones, that I hear on TV whilst typing. Every now and then, I look up in amazement because somebody on TV is saying the exact word or phrase that I am typing at that very moment. It's bad when typing "toxic relationships" and hearing it reverberating in my head, or suddenly being struck by "cancer research" or "vengeance."

What is the most absurd question someone has asked you about England?

I have just read this question, a bit late, but it is one of my favorite topics.

I am from London, and since moving to the States in 1990 I have lived in South Texas for 30 of those years. I love it here, and couldn't stand the cold, drizzly days in England again. However, I have had so many weird questions asked about me, and England, I can't even begin to enumerate them.

Here's a few:

"Are you from Britain?"

...Wow, that's amazing for starters. I usually get, are you from Canada, Australia, New Zealand, Germany, Ireland

and even South Africa, which I think is stretching it a bit too far.

"Yes, I'm from England."

Puzzled look. "Is that the capital city of Paris?"

… I try to explain that Paris is in France, which is a totally different country, but am interrupted by,

"What language do they speak in England?"

… If you think this is being cute, think again, and as somebody else wondered if it was sarcasm, I can assure you that it is not.

"Do you have tea with the Queen?" another asks, quite seriously.

… Hmm! "Er, no, she doesn't like chocolate digestive biscuits."

… Really puzzled look because in Texas biscuits are little round, flaky pastry cakes served hot with brown gravy on top. They are definitely not cookies.

"Surely you don't put gravy on chocolate biscuits. They would taste funny and probably melt."

… And so it goes until I am exasperated and walk away.

Oh, how about when I say I am from London and some poor soul asks, "London, Texas?"

Now it is me with the cross-eyes. I think that they must be really kidding me. London, Texas is a one-horse town (which means it is agricultural farmland, practically on the edge of the desert). Do I really sound that Texan? I don't think so.

While sorting through a deceased person's possessions what is the most disturbing thing you found?

When my husband committed suicide 23 years ago, I was so angry because I had no idea why he had done it.

I went through his clothes and put them and his shoes in a big, black bag to take to Goodwill. When I put my hand in one of the pockets, I found his wallet. I looked inside and found a love letter from a girl he had often talked about when we were married. The letter was written to him many years ago. In fact, he had carried it close to his heart throughout our 18-year marriage.

I found that most disturbing.

Why don't very old people seem to get bored?

There comes a time in most people's lives when they realize that they no longer want to change the world.

For some there was a very painful period before this realization when they felt tremendous guilt because they were not out there making a difference with the best of them. It is a settling in period which causes some distress. Settling into old age is not something people desire.

The way of life in the West is competition. You see it everywhere, and you expect to see it on TV all the time. Everything is a competition. Everybody wants to win. It is the natural order of things in this go- getting world we live in. No chance for resting on your laurels when you are young. You are judged by what you do, not by who you are.

People think that older people should be busy doing things all the time. Before this acceptance settles in, older people like to be busy. They do their best to learn everything that they would do if they were younger. Technology is a fine example. It passes a lot of time in old age, and many people find this a time to better themselves and keep up with the grandchildren.

But when this mindset changes, and they have got past the guilt, it is a relief to find out that they are really quite happy with who they are. There is no need to prove yourself to anybody. You realize you are a human being and not a human doing.

Arriving at that realization takes a great deal of maturity. It seems unnatural at first, but it is the most natural way to live at the end of one's life.

Once people have accepted their contentment with what is, there is no chance of boredom. Life is not about passing time in a positive manner; it is about being who you are and happy.

If you think of animals, they don't worry about being bored. The days pass, and time is of no consequence. Cows stand in the field chewing the cud, and monkeys play all day without guilt.

It is not even a question of memories. Yes, it is nice to have good memories, but that is not what older people spend their day thinking about. They think about bodily functions like eating and sleeping. These things, and their illnesses, become all important in very old age.

I just want to be me and do what I want to do. I find myself getting addicted to puzzles and card games and do feel guilty. It is my guilty secret. However, when I reason with myself, I see that there is no harm in doing puzzles and playing card games, and I don't need to answer to anybody.

This is a very difficult period, one of great guilt, but I am working towards acceptance and shall soon be content to take down my shingle and enjoy my dinner!

How can people tell if you are not confident in yourself?

Here is the dictionary's definition of self-confidence:

"A feeling of self-assurance arising from one's appreciation of one's own abilities or qualities. She's brimming with confidence."

A lack of confidence has a lot to do with shame. If somebody in your life has made you feel ashamed of yourself, you will not look people in the eye and walk with your head down. Shame is not the same as guilt as it goes much deeper than that. Guilt is when you feel bad about something you have done. It is not a reflection on yourself as a person. But when you suffer from shame, it is not that you have done something wrong, it is that you are not fit to walk the earth. Someone has made you feel that you are not a fit human being. You are a damaged person.

People who are confident in themselves don't have a problem, and more than likely don't even question it.

I personally think confidence, like so many other things, comes from our childhood. If you were brought up in a family that praised you and celebrated your wins and achievements, it usually follows that you would be more than confident in yourself. Approval is a wonderful gift to give a child.

Yet so many families are only too willing to withhold approval from their children. This produces insecure adults who are always seeking their parents' approval. This can go on throughout their adult years, and if nothing positive takes its place, this lack of approval will continue to affect a person until they die.

If, on the other hand, your parents approve of you and the things you do, it is highly likely that you have a more successful life than people who are disapproved of.

It is true, you can gain confidence in your life by doing something you feel proud of. You don't need anybody else's approval. If you feel good about yourself that is enough.

It doesn't really matter what you do, it can be as small as arranging a bouquet of flowers. If you feel proud of what you achieved, it can give you confidence. You might even go on to work in a flower shop, which would raise your confidence level even higher.

I spent my life living with a lack of self-confidence. And that was, once again, because of my childhood. I was not encouraged to do anything. Even if I did well at something, I was not praised, it went unnoticed. All this adds up to a lack of confidence, and that was the story of my life.

I slowly built up my confidence by writing on Quora and have now written over 5,000 answers to many and varied questions. Whether they are well received or not doesn't matter as I am happy that I am able to write down what I feel and hopefully help other people in the process.

One day, a woman who read my work on Quora suggested that I write a book. I didn't believe I could do that because I had never been told I could do anything like that before. However, I decided to take her up on it and have since written 9 books which have all been published.

This has given me tremendous self-confidence and I don't think I shall ever look back.

So, it is all about throwing off your upbringing, having faith in yourself and doing something challenging. If you have a mentor all the better. I had to wait until I was 73 to find a mentor, but I am so happy that I did.

What are some useful things that people learn too late in life or never at all?

This is another one of those questions (a great one, by the way) that could easily take a book to answer. There are so many useful things that people learn too late in life, or never at all.

I have a really great therapist and have been lucky enough to be on the receiving end of his wisdom for the past 23 years. Some people say that is a long time in therapy, but I would have to disagree as I learn new things or brush up on old things I failed to learn, every time I see him.

One of the things that is very useful to know is people come into our lives at the appropriate time to teach us what we need to know to advance our personal growth.

Yesterday, I told my therapist about my friend who never has a good word to say to me. We write often, but I never share my secrets or my feelings with him because I know that he will make fun of me and make me feel bad.

Last week, for example, I sent him a copy of some drawings I had done, and he wrote back and said that most of them were quite good, but one of them looked like a petulant schoolgirl had drawn it.

Well!

Do you think I took any notice of the ones he liked? Not on your life. I could only dwell on the one he didn't like.

When I told my therapist this sorry tale, he said that my so-called friend had come into my life for a reason, and that was to work on my personal growth. I was stunned. Until that time, I had thought of him as just a friend, but as my therapist was quick to point out, a friend is someone who encourages you and you feel you can be yourself with without ridicule. I had to agree with that.

"So, why should I keep in touch with him?" I asked my therapist, naively.

"You need to keep in touch with him because he is a gift in your life and there for your personal growth!"

Now, this is old news to me. I have been told this, and recognized the truth in it, hundreds of times before but here was the situation again and I was being faced to look at it.

Apparently, as I should know by now, my friend has a very shaky ego and needs me to bolster his feelings about himself.

Ah, ha!

And as I should also know, my friend, the gift in my life, is here to help me understand my own failings. Simple as that. Then, the embarrassing bit is I have to face the fact that my shaky ego needs the occasional boosting, too, and I am not quite as nice as I thought I was sometimes.

Now, this kind of information really stings! Ouch!

Yet that is the kind of thing most people never get to learn about in their whole lives. They go to their death bed thinking that they didn't need relationships with people like my friend, but I can now see the error in that kind of thinking.

Now, I shall be on the lookout for anything else I have yet to learn about myself through my relationship with this friend. He may be somebody I would want to give the push, but he is in fact very useful in my life.

You might try asking yourself what all those undesirable people are in your life for? What are they trying to teach you?

If I can be brave enough to admit my failings, so can you.

I hate everything about myself. How do I start loving myself more?

Leaning to love yourself is a tall order. It takes years of practice, especially when you start with hate. Yet many people say they hate themselves. Where does all this hate come from? Why are we feeling so bad about ourselves?

Can you see how devastating to the human spirit this is? With this attitude, you can barely hold your head up, let alone be comfortable talking to other people. Hate keeps you from living the life of your dreams.

So how can you get rid of all this hate?

If I was to say, just stop hating yourself, you would probably laugh because it is easier said than done. How can you throw away an opinion you have had of yourself for most of your life? Remember this, babies never hate themselves. It is learned behavior.

If it is learned behavior, who taught you to hate yourself, and why did you listen to them? If you hate yourself so much, it is very likely that you have had a lot of practice at this and you have been doing it most of your life. Maybe ever since you were a little child. Yet you did not grow up hating yourself for no reason.

It is highly likely that your parents or teachers taught you how to hate yourself. And you listened because they were the authority in your life.

If somebody keeps pointing out all the things you have done wrong (in their eyes) you begin to believe them and eventually take on this position about yourself. "My mother says I am rubbish, stupid, fat and lazy so I must be." We usually listen to what our parents say about us and believe them.

If someone kept telling me I amounted to nothing, I would learn to hate myself, too. In fact, that was the case when I grew up. But I have overcome that now.

The way I overcame it is not to take the giant leap from hate to love. We cannot expect to do that. If you were learning to high jump, you would not put the bar 6 foot high off the ground. You would have to work up to that, putting the bar up in increments as you learn.

It is the same with these awful opinions we have of ourselves. We cannot go from hate to love in one fell swoop, we must learn to like ourselves first. Liking yourself is much easier than loving yourself. You like a lot of people. You have friends who you like very much. You like your pets and your hobbies.

It is now time to practice liking yourself. You can do this in increments, like raising the high jump bar. Learn to like the way you smile, or cook a meal, or are kind to animals. Find new things you like about yourself every day. Practice, practice, practice. Soon enough you will see that you are quite a likable person. You can even list all the things you like about yourself in a notebook if that helps.

Now is the time to learn to love yourself.

Loving yourself is an act of kindness. It is more than liking yourself. It is where you work at taking care of your basic needs. We all need shelter, warmth, food to eat, water to drink, and clothes to cover our bodies.

These are the basic things you need if you are to love yourself. Stop making do with rubbish and give yourself something you can be proud of. Make sure you have a nice place to live, or if that is not possible, find a nice, comfy room or even the corner of a room all to yourself.

Once you are comfortable in your surroundings, be sure to eat properly, which does not mean junk food. Shop on the periphery of the store and buy good food, not processed food which is bad for your body and your brain. Be sure to get enough to drink and buy nice clothes to wear. Do you get the picture? Suddenly you have gone from hating yourself to loving yourself so much that you have become a good provider for yourself.

With this attitude you will go far. Stop judging yourself and praise yourself instead. Judging is painful, so it is not good for you. It is something only people who hate themselves do.

Look around you and do all the things that are good for you. Walk in the park, take a drive, eat ice cream. No matter what it is, do things that show you love yourself.

I live far away from my family and there is nobody to share my feelings with. I have friends but they aren't interested in my feelings. What should I do?

You are like me. You are a feeling type of person. You mentioned feelings twice in your question. The first thing to do is to sort out your feelings from the facts.

You can't feel alone, but you can feel lonely. Being alone is just a fact. Like I have dark hair and blue eyes. These are facts. Being alone is another fact.

However, I certainly see your dilemma as you are stuck with your feelings, and nobody wants to hear about them.

The world is full of thinkers. Thinkers think and they rarely feel, or at least they rarely share their feelings with other people. So, you seem to be stuck with all these thinkers. I know what you mean. I tend to be surrounded by thinkers who don't share my feelings either.

Once upon a time, I used to try to share my feelings with all these thinkers, but when I saw it was a waste of time, I stopped and kept my feelings to myself. People generally are not interested in other people's feelings. They often find them embarrassing, or just too much to handle. And some people think about how they are feeling when you mention your feelings, and they are often shocked at how bad they feel themselves.

The thing to do is to share your feelings with something safe like a journal. Journals are hardy souls. They do not care how much you share your feelings with them because they never get upset. A journal is a fine way to cope with your feelings because you can pour your heart out and it doesn't matter. Your journal will always love you no matter how bad you feel.

Another thing that is great for sharing feelings with is a pet. Pets love you, come rain or shine, and just love to listen to all your secrets. See if you can find a pet who you can share your feelings with.

I have cats and they know how I feel about everything because I take them into my confidence. They are great secret-keepers, too. We have our little secrets together.

So, my advice to you is to stop trying to share your feelings with all these thinking types and find another way to share how you feel. Good luck.

Is 39 considered old? I have so much to accomplish, and I want to travel and enjoy life more, but I feel too old.

Look at it this way, if I was 21, I would consider you very old, but as I am 76 I consider you very young! Do you understand?

Now, let me look at my life at 39 and see what I did after that to make my life interesting.

At 39, I retired from nursing, sold my bed and breakfast in Cornwall, England and came to America. Here we bought an RV and toured the country for 6 years full time. It was a wonderful adventure.

At 45, we sold our RV, flew to Amsterdam, bought another RV, and toured Europe for 6 months. That was a huge adventure.

At 46, we returned to America and moved to Texas. It is here where my husband died.

Since then, I have been living the best life possible on my own. Never regretted a day. I write, I paint, and generally have a great time being retired and my own boss.

Between the ages of 55 and now, I have been to Australia three times, Costa Rica, Malta, England, and many places in the U.S. Now I am quite happy to settle down and put my traveling days behind me.

AT 73 I published my first book.

At 76 I have published 9 books, and they are all on Amazon.

So, from my point of view, your life at 39 has just begun. Go out there and enjoy it.

How can I find happiness if I am unhappy in life?

Now let's see, where have I found all this happiness that seems to have evaded you? I'll put on my 'Search for Happiness' glasses and have a look around.

First things first. What are the basic requirements for happiness?

Family

Oh, dear, I haven't done well at all on that score. My glasses are steamed up already. Parents both dead by the time I was 15, only brother in Australia 10,000 miles away. Only child dead, no grandchildren. Alone in a foreign country. Not a very good start, eh?

Love

That one really does take a nosedive, I can assure you. 3 rotten marriages, 2 divorces, 1 suicide. 1 died of Covid. I don't think I am marriage material at all. No bosom buddies to speak of, either.

Health

Now you'd think I was fine to look at me, but that is a wonky picture. Bipolar Disorder all my life cannot be explained if you haven't been there, but what a merry dance that has led me. Not to mention all the physical ailments, but I won't even go into that.

Money

Now you've really got me, I can hardly see out of my glasses at all. "Money doesn't grow on trees," my mother told me, and she was right. Social Security comes in handy, but you can't do much on that.

Faith

Nope. Not at all lucky in that department, either. Tried every church in town, never fitted in anywhere.

So, what does that leave me with? I'll put down my glasses and see what's going on today.

I woke up this morning with my usual backache, could hardly bend down to feed the cat. Had a spinal epidural only last week. That didn't work. Still alone and broke. Nothing changed there. Haven't been anywhere or seen anyone for months due to Covid.

But I am happy. Annoyingly, irritatingly happy.

Happiness is a choice. We can choose to be happy, or we can choose to be miserable. We get to decide. You choose what to wear and what to eat every day, don't you? Happiness is just the same. You can't find it on the outside, even with the most expensive glasses, because happiness comes from within.

Sit down and smile.

Yes, smile. I know it is difficult, but you would never believe what it does for your morale. Force the corners of your mouth to turn upwards, if you have to. Happiness lives somewhere behind that smile. Just try it.

How can you avoid feeling that everything in your life has been insignificant?

There is something wrong with your sentence. What you describe is a thought not a feeling.

How can you avoid thinking everything in your lifetime is insignificant is a thought. Now you need to ask yourself how that statement makes you feel. That I cannot answer for you.

Does this insignificance make you sad, mad, glad, sorry, angry, or what?

Feelings (emotions) follow thoughts. So, if you examine your thought, you might realize that you can change it. Then if you manage to change your thought, your feelings will change as well.

If I said, my life has been hell, this would be a generalization like the word, insignificant. I could go through my life thinking my life was hell and feeling angry or sad about it, but if I started to look closely at my life, I might remember what a great time I had on holiday in Athens when I was 25. That certainly wasn't hell. Then I might remember another couple of times when I was happy, glad, exuberant, joyful because my life has obviously not been hell for years and years.

So, it is with your thought. Change it. Think about all the things, no matter how small, that were significant in your life, and you will have instantly changed your thought.

Then see how you feel about your new life.

How does a person heal from childhood trauma?

If you think of childhood trauma, or any other trauma, as a gaping wound you will more easily see how to heal it.

If it is a small wound, you may be able to deal with it yourself, but if it is an open wound it may need stitches in the form of therapy.

You will need to leave the stitches in for a long time for it to heal properly, so you will need to do therapy for a long time as well; longer if the wound was deep. It might even have been a puncture wound in which case it will be very painful and take a very long time to heal.

Once the stitches come out, there might be a scab formed where the wound had once been. Scabs do heal but not if you keep picking at them, so it is best to not keep going over and over the trauma and making yourself ill by opening up the old wound again.

If you leave the scab to heal you may well be left with a scar. That is your badge of honor to say that you have survived your trauma. Keep looking at your scar every day and congratulate yourself for having done the therapy and the work it required to heal your childhood wound.

Can you learn to be more spiritual in the same way you learn about facts, or is it more of a heart thing?

Thank you for your question. Yes, you can learn to be more spiritual, but not in the same way as you learn facts.

When you learn facts, you are calling on your memory which is a left-brain function, whereas with learning spiritual lessons you are calling on your observation which belongs to the right brain. Observation takes a great deal more effort than does learning that two plus two equals four.

There is a movement called stalking in which a person becomes hyper-vigilant to patterns that are the product of the right brain. As there are millions of facts in this world so there are millions of spiritual lessons to be learned so it is easier to tackle them one at a time.

Let's work spiritually on one example:

What causes the constant chatter that goes on in everybody's mind all day?

In India this is called The Chattering Monkey on your Shoulder. Others call it various names like The Shadow, The Devil, even The Unwelcome Guest. I like to call it the Parasite because it lives inside your mind which it uses as a host.

The parasite talks to you all the time. He says things like, "You stupid idiot, why did you do that?" or "Don't you realize how fat you look in that dress?" or "Look at you, making a fool of yourself again."

As you will notice the Parasite is never polite or kind, in fact he is also known as The Judge. He sits there in your mind all day and judges everything you do. This can be very upsetting, and most of the world has no idea how to control The Parasite without meditating 24/7.

One way to catch this Judge is to stalk him. This means whenever you hear a little voice in your head judging you, take note. Be aware. Then tell your judge that you are not interested in his opinion, you are doing perfectly fine on your own, thank you.

This is very alarming to the Parasite as he is suddenly deprived of food (your sadness at being judged). The more you listen to him, the more he eats your thoughts, and the fatter he gets.

If you look at this in a spiritual light, you will begin to see that it is not you that is judging, it is in fact your mind playing tricks on you. If you can catch it before it becomes upsetting, you will have learned an enormous spiritual lesson.

Learning facts, as you can see, is nowhere near as difficult as practicing spiritual lessons.

I leave you with this practice. It is now up to you to stalk your Parasite.

How did your marriage end?

This is an old question, but I think it would do me good to answer it and try to make sense of my husband's suicide.

Let's be clear from the start. Our marriage was not a happy one most of the time. We were not living happily at all. And when people talk about losing a loved one, this did not apply to me. That in itself set me apart from all the other grieving widows at the Grief group I went to. I was shunned by everybody due to my husband's suicide. They simply turned their backs on me.

Controlling behavior and bipolar disorder

Our marriage had been wonderful at first, then the 18 years his controlling behavior took over and ruined what we once had. We started off with a bang, all flowers and champagne. Then just as suddenly all that dissolved into sheer terror for me.

I have bipolar disorder and that in itself had a dreadful effect on our marriage and our happiness. My moods were fine for the first 11 years of our marriage, then with menopause, all hell broke loose, and I was not a wonderful partner to be married to, I am quite sure.

With this, the controlling grew more and more insistent. What had started out as my fierce independence, ended up over the years with me being totally at the mercy of the iron claw. The situation was dire. It became either him or me, and he decided to end his own life.

Everyday life under my husband's control

I was not allowed out of the house on my own, and in fact I was locked in my house when he went out. I was not allowed to buy anything at all without his permission, so even purchasing a new lipstick was grounds for a tribunal. All the outings were joint, and shopping was a nightmare as I was as good as a dog on a leash being tugged in his direction should I stray. "Sally where are you?" if I so much as stopped to look at the price of apples. Then the tug - return to his side. My emails and my phone calls were timed and vetted, my family and social circle closed up so tight I could barely breathe. And after his death, I realized that I didn't even have a key to my own house. Using his, my hand shook so much I could hardly open the door.

So, as you can see, the situation was very strange to say the least - my illness and his control.

Mental hospital

There were many events leading up to his death, but the most important one for sure was my admittance to hospital. Don't get me wrong. That was not the first or the last time I have been in a mental hospital. In fact, I have spent 14 months of my life in mental hospitals, so I was no stranger that time.

He had attachment disorder, according to a psychiatric report when he once threatened to kill himself, so my going away sent him into a total panic. He was up at the hospital all the time, terrified I might disappear and not come home. He bugged the staff, even the psychiatrist by slipping little notes in his pocket when he passed on his rounds. He was told to leave and not come back.

The suicide

I stayed in for a month - and even then, was totally psychotic and should never have been let out at all. Then the day, and the exact time, I was due to be released, my husband decided was the right time to kill himself so he wrote me a note stating the time 2 pm feeling bad now, 2.30 drifting off, 3.00 don't think I shall make it, then scrawl like a little bird running across the page and ending mid-sentence. Gone.

Things did not go according to plan for my husband. I did not go home. My friend picked me up from the hospital and took me straight to her house. I was not fit to be out of hospital, so was in a dreadful state, and just slept for hours and hours.

Two days passed, no word from him. My friend had to go away so she took me to a halfway house where people go as a transitional sanctuary from hospital to home. My psychosis was bad. I thought I had bugs crawling all over my room and had to keep getting out the vacuum to clean the bathroom because of all the bugs that kept appearing every time I went in there.

Finally going home

Then two more days passed. I hadn't heard from him, and

a couple of friends took me to my house to see what was happening.

When we drove up, there were six police cars outside, and uniformed officers milling about everywhere. I had no idea what was going on. Then a police man came up to the car and told me that my husband had committed suicide. I remember keening in the back seat, rocking back and forth, a high-pitched sound like a wounded animal coming out of my mouth.

You will have to bear with me because the days after that were spent in a dream. My friend took care of me and arranged everything. You will never understand how I felt, because it is impossible to fathom how sick a person with bipolar can be under such stress. I was there, that's all I know. I was there.

The fall out

To say he left me in a mess is an understatement. He had $6,000 in credit card debt and I was far too ill to work. He had sent his pension to the lost dog's home; left me such disgusting illustrated emails I cannot bring myself to tell you. Also, he had given away thirteen of my framed oil paintings. It took me 5 years of rage to get over the loss of my paintings.

Weeks were spent in a trance, unable to move, lying on my back on the couch all day, pinned down by a heavy tombstone on my chest. I had to relearn how to drive a car, be accompanied to the bank, taught how to write a check, shown how to pay the household bills. I was a mess.

Loss of autonomy

The worst part of the whole experience was I had to regain my autonomy as a person. If you have never lost your autonomy, you cannot imagine how difficult it is to live. I felt totally ill equipped to make any decisions at all, even the simplest things like what to eat. Every time I went to buy anything, I felt him standing behind me looking over my shoulder.

I was taken by my friend to my current psychotherapist, and from that time on I was taught how to climb out of my mess. My therapist told me he was surprised to see me there at all because he expected me to be either dead or in prison. The fate of many women in my position.

However, the human spirit wins out in the end. Twenty-three years later I have not only survived, but thrived, and I am here to help others pass through the gates of hell.

Thank you for reading to the end.

What has your life been like?

I am nearly 77 and my life has changed for the better.

I know it is fashionable to talk about how dreadful things are, how many illnesses you have, how nobody likes you, but I am through with all that. I just want to be happy. And I am happy, living alone with my two cats.

My life has been one long adventure, and I could tell you tales that would make your hair stand on end. I have been there, done that, suffered like the rest of them, but what good does it do to keep moaning and complaining about everything? I certainly don't want any more of that.

My three marriages went down the toilet. I never had the kids I wanted, so no grandkids either. My health is shot, both physically and mentally, I have nothing in the bank, but I have my freedom, and that's all I want.

When I was small my mother was always ill, and I was the one who had to take care of her, so my care-taking role began very early in life and has carried me through to today. Naturally, being the good caretaker that I was, I chose a career in nursing and took care of hundreds and hundreds of people for years.

I married three abusers, and I took care of them, too. I was a puppet on a string at their beck and call. I sat up at nights until 4 am when the casinos closed and my gambling husband came up stairs to bed, treading softly if he had lost, bounding up two steps at a time, Champagne on ice if he had won.

Then there were the other women. The phone calls at dinner, the quick getaways, the weekends in London. And me, the naive caretaker, driving him to Glasgow airport thinking he was going on some weekend business conference. Give me a break.

And a break I got.

I just want to be by myself. I like my own company and don't crave anything. I prefer nature and animals to people.

I no longer wait for some errant husband to buy me flowers.
I buy bunches and bunches of flowers to make myself happy.
Freedom is a fine thing.

What is the best way to deal with hatred of someone?

Hatred is a very difficult emotion to deal with.

Hatred is so strong that it can take over your life. In the end it harms nobody but you. The other person can have no idea how much you hate them. It is only you who is suffering.

It is a spiritual dilemma.

Just like envy and jealousy, hatred is a great burden to carry.

If you look at this in purely spiritual terms you will discover that you are taking on the position of judge and jury. You have decided for yourself that this person does not deserve your love. What gives you that right?

Nothing does.

Also, you are judging yourself. Perhaps more so. Even your question states that this is true. Judging yourself is very hard on the spirit. It can cut you to the quick. Every day of your life, spiritually speaking, you are walking around with the judge's hat on. Judging yourself even more harshly than others.

So now, we are looking at this in a very different way. We are in fact looking into a mirror. You are projecting your self-hatred onto another. So, you must search your soul and ask yourself why you hate yourself so much. It may seem odd, but your hatred of yourself is what is really causing you so much pain.

Somehow, you will have to learn to love yourself and this can be the biggest challenge of your life.

The way to love is forgiveness.

You will need to examine all the things you hate about yourself, then learn to forgive them once and for all.

You have a very long spiritual road ahead of you because one of the hardest things you will ever have to do in life is to love yourself. There is no short cut. It comes through forgiveness.

Forgive this person who is upsetting you and concentrate on loving yourself.

How can we help someone who is very depressed? What should we never do?

The strange thing is, the more serious the depression, the less you can help. Now that's a peculiar thought, but I shall tell you why.

When a person is just going into a depression, he is still amenable to discussion. He may be upset because he is unable to work due to the lack of motivation which comes with depression. He may also be upset that he is unable to fulfill his role in the family. But he may be able to tell you how he is feeling which may help you understand.

A person who is suffering from these feelings is overcome with guilt. Depression brings not only sadness and thoughts of worthlessness, but an overwhelming sense of guilt.

There doesn't have to be any reason for the guilt, but a depressed person will feel it acutely in any case. The thing you can do to help a depressed person who is suffering from guilt is to not put any pressure on them to act.

They will have very little energy, as depression is draining. Trying to force them to do things can be extremely burdensome. The kindest thing to do is to encourage them to rest. Rest is good for depression. It lessens the chance of the depression getting worse because the body and the mind needs to rest.

It is just like the flu. You wouldn't expect a person to get up and go to work if they had the flu. You would let them stay home, go to bed, and rest. If you can encourage them to do that, you would be alleviating the dreadful burden of guilt. Make them some small meals and encourage them to drink some water. Be kind and do not push.

You can also be very helpful if you encourage the person to get medical help in the form of medication. Unfortunately, it takes at least two weeks for anti-depressants to work so there won't be immediate improvement.

Now, should a person's depression get worse, it becomes really difficult to get through to them. Motivation to do anything will be gone, so it is no use trying to push them to do things. Energy will be at an all-time low. It will be enough for a severely depressed person to walk across the room.

And should the depression really worsen they will be unable to get out of bed. That is very frustrating for somebody who wants to help, but nagging will do not good and only exacerbate the problems.

It is best to gently encourage the person to do what they can. Once they are out of bed, it will be kind to not nag them to shower as the energy it takes to shower is enormous and can only be appreciated by someone who is far too depressed to even brush their teeth.

I have often been severely depressed, and putting the toothpaste on the toothbrush was too much for me. Besides when you are that depressed, you cannot understand what needs to be done because your mind will not be working properly, and you will be confused.

So, the best thing to do with a depressed person is to try to halt the illness before it sets in by getting them to the doctor in order to start medication. And then appreciating that they will need to rest.

What should we never do?

The worst things you can say are:

"You have everything going for you, you shouldn't be depressed."

"Buck up now."

"Come on, make some effort."

"Snap out of it."

Believe me, if the person could just snap out of it, they would have done so long ago because the pain of depression is unrelenting and unbearable.

But it is good that you want to help, and I applaud you for that. It is very difficult to sit back and watch a person deteriorate. But your job is to encourage and not to nag.

When I started to return to normal, my doctor told me to just do one thing a day. I was told to put the laundry in the washing machine and turn it on. Then the next day put it in the drier.

That may seem really strange to you who would think nothing of doing the laundry. But believe me when you are seriously depressed it is more than enough. So be kind, encourage them, and try to relieve the burden of guilt.

Does life just happen to you?

I have always envied people who can plan their lives. It seems such a cool way to live. Imagine knowing what you would be doing next year, or even some time way off in the future. I admire these people but have no idea how they do it.

My therapist says I am a wild spirit. A leaf at the mercy of the wind.

I used to think that was funny, but I can't tell you how many times I have regretted drifting about on the breeze. I now think of myself as a piece of flotsam bouncing about in the windy desert. You see thousands of them by the wayside in Arizona stuck to a barbed wire fence.

That has always been my lot in life. "Just wait and see what happens."

Let's see, what has happened to me?

Oh, yes, I remember the time when I met husband #2. That was a fiasco of amazing proportions, and I can't think of anyone who would be stupid enough to do what I did.

We met when we were both selling encyclopedias door to door in London. He was from Malta, and I found him irresistible. The in-love stage hit me hard, and before I knew it, I had cashed in my lucrative job, vacated my little basement flat, and left for Malta. I had no idea where Malta was at the time but assumed that if he came from there it must be wonderful. I didn't even think to look it up on the map.

All I knew was how romantic it was to drive south down the backbone of Europe in his white Fiat sports car. The sun was shining, and we were in love. It didn't occur to me how I would get back to England someday. If indeed I would ever get back to England at all!

I certainly never imagined that the guy who filled the gas tank in Naples would whip my only suitcase off the top of the car. And worse, my new lover would refuse to go back and get it, leaving me with the clothes I stood up in. (You can probably guess what was in the suitcase. It took me many years to realize it.)

I never considered I might be stranded in a foreign country

minus my inheritance that I had entrusted to the new love of my life. (He blew that on the second day in the casino in Monte Carlo!)

And guess what? I was stranded in a foreign country one day when we had a fight and he left me standing by the roadside in a strange town in Malta. I am just grateful that his conscience got the better of him, and he came back to get me.

But that was a long time ago, when I was really young.

The only problem is I seem to have made hasty exists all my life, never thinking of the consequences. I only have myself to blame.

What about the time, many years later, when I sold my quaint house in Cornwall, not a thought about what I, or my American husband (#3), would do next. I must have had some vague notion of returning to England at some time in the distant future, but there were no plans.

We sold everything in Cornwall, and I even allowed myself to be persuaded to cash in my nursing pension. (I thought about that 20 years later when I was struggling to make ends meet in a little town in Texas).

And what about when we had toured America and Europe,

then found ourselves six years later stuck like the flotsam in the desert, though this time it was in Amsterdam in the winter.

What to do next? Oh, no, we found out that it was impossible to get back to England without submitting our golden Labrador, Ziggy, to six grueling months in quarantine. So, we came back to America.

Do you think I even considered that husband #3, who was 16 years older than me, would die by suicide at 70 leaving me stranded in America? Never crossed my mind. But I knew all about it when he did and have been stuck like flotsam to the fence ever since.

So, all you life-planners out there - just sink your anchors into the ocean and make me jealous.

What advice can you give to lonely people?

Unfortunately, I have experienced many years of loneliness myself, and know from personal experience how soul-destroying it is.

Many people have no clue what loneliness is all about. They blithely say things like, "Oh, I lived on my own for 6 months and I was never lonely." I say, lucky you, to these people. They have no idea what loneliness feels like, and I am happy for them.

The point is, if you have a life outside of yourself and your four walls, then you have no reason to be lonely. If those people who think they are lonely have friends, or a loving family who keeps in touch with them, they are not likely to be lonely. Just being by yourself for a few hours a day does not equal loneliness.

It is really alarming to know how many people are in despair. They feel lonely, unloved and think they will lose their minds if their loneliness doesn't stop.

I think loneliness is like a bug, like a Pandemic even, millions of people the world over are suffering from this virus. It's not like you can go to the pharmacy and get a shot for loneliness like you can get a shot for the flu. Wouldn't that be nice? We could then kiss loneliness goodbye.

But life is just not like that, people are lonely and that's that.

I am desperately floundering around here, because I feel as if I should be able to account for the way I cured my loneliness, but I can't really pinpoint it, or come up with a course you could follow. In fact, it would be great if you could take a course online "Cure for Loneliness,' but so far, I haven't come across a course like that.

If there is no shot and no course we can rely on, then we seem to be left to our own devices to climb out of this black pit of loneliness.

"How did I move from lonely to happy with my own company?" I keep asking myself that question. The last time I spoke to my brother in Australia, he said, "Do you ever get lonely?" I had to think for a moment, then said, "I used to, but not anymore."

My life is now really busy with writing, (I have now written 9 books in the past 3 years), and the goals I never dared to dream of before have materialized in my 70s. So how on earth did I cure my loneliness? I have no idea.

All I can say is that loneliness can be temporary, and it is possible to eventually climb out of that black pit and feel content with being alone. They are two very different things - being alone and being lonely - but you don't need me to tell you that.

Loneliness is extremely painful, but there is hope out there. And there really is a light at the end of the tunnel.

How horrible is depression?

Depression is a devastating illness that changes who you are. It is horrible. It is always horrible. Anybody who tells you otherwise is lying.

Depression is always horrible for one reason, and I will tell you what that is:

When you are depressed, you start to lose hope of ever getting well again. And we all need hope to cling to.

Depression is a progressive illness. It starts out with feeling tired and maybe a little irritable, but soon progresses into a feeling of sadness and hopelessness. Your head feels like it is full of cotton wool, and you can no longer do the things you used to take for granted.

You slowly begin to realize that you are not fit for this world and start to think you'll never get better. You get desperate. It feels like drowning. You would kick and scream if you had the energy. But you don't.

Soon enough, you start to feel like a failure. You are so tired you cannot do the things you used to do, including doing your job and looking after your family. And, if you would admit it to yourself, you no longer want to live. In fact, all you can think about now is death and dying. You think you would be doing your family a favor if you killed yourself, but you just don't have the energy to make a plan.

Now hopelessness is really settling in.

You find you have no energy to take a shower, and no desire to take a shower either. People try to help, but you know in your heart that nothing can help you. You might as well give up. When you finally lose hope, you just want to die. That is how horrible depression really is.

When did you stop caring what other people thought about you?

To be very honest I cared what other people thought of me up until about three years ago. I am now 76, so you can see what a late start I got.

Caring what others think of you is the normal human condition and it takes a certain trigger to realize that it is a fool-hardy way to live. In my case, it took many years of therapy to realize some things in my life weren't working at all.

The problem is we always take things personally. It's a natural thing to do.

We get hurt all the time.

Other people's opinions about us are just that, opinions.

They may be bad; they may be good. Whatever they are the trick is to not take them personally. Even when somebody tells you they think you are great, it is only their opinion. Take no notice.

Let other people's opinions pass through you like smoke, then you will no longer care what people think of you.

How should I reply to "How are you," When I'm not fine at all?

When I was going through an extremely hard patch, I was faced with that same problem. One thing I know is that for the majority of people "How are you?" is just a meaningless saying. They are not really interested in how you are because they have their own hangups and problems.

I asked my therapist that very same question and he said, if you don't know somebody well just say, "I've been better."

This has worked for me every time. Some people come back and take an interest in what is really wrong with you, while others say, "Oh, I am sorry to hear that." Either way, it is a natural response to a meaningless question.

One caveat, though, don't go launching into an hour-long

monologue about your latest operation or your daughter's problems in school. People really don't want to know all the details unless they ask. And nobody wants to be stuck listening to your problems and unable to get away.

I'm sure you have met people before who have these monologues. I can name quite a few people I know. But when these long one-sided 'conversations' take place, I leave as quickly as I can.

So only tell people your problems if they are genuinely interested, but don't expect them to give you any answers.

Nobody truly understands me, not even my family or friends. I always feel that I'm alone all the time, and I have to face every problem on my own? How can I feel better?

I have found that the majority of the human race feels misunderstood. Everybody thinks others should understand them when, in actual fact, they do not really understand themselves.

I wonder if you truly understand yourself. Are you familiar with your good points and your failings? Do you try to correct your failings or just live with them? If you don't understand yourself, it is unreasonable to expect others to understand you at all.

Even if you have lived with people for many years, it is doubtful you will understand them either. Do you know what other people are thinking? Can you mind read? If you can then you are the exception to the rule. Most people have no idea what is going on in another person's mind, even if they think they know the person well.

Did your parents understand you? Did you understand them? When you were young, you were changing all the time, so how could you expect anyone to understand you. And you surely didn't understand yourself.

How many partners really understand each other? It is likely that they are always doing things that are unfathomable. We are all a mixed bag of conflicting ideas and opinions. One day we think one way, the next day we change our minds and think something quite different.

It is unreasonable to think others should understand us, isn't it?

You also say you don't like facing problems alone. I think a lot of people would agree with you about that. It is much nicer to have someone else to talk things over with. Sometimes, two minds are better than one. But life isn't like that. Sometimes, you have to get on with it.

I am alone, like you, and hate making big decisions on my own, but the truth is, my husband is gone, so I must accept my situation. It is no use pretending that it should be otherwise. This is what it is, and nothing can change it.

Sadly, the same thing applies to you. We are alone, even when we are surrounded by other people. We are alone with our thoughts and feelings, and we cannot expect others to understand us at all.

What life situation took you a long time to understand?

There are many life situations that took me a long time to understand, but I suppose the most important one is that I much prefer my own company to being with other people no matter who they are.

It may be nice for some people to have others to talk to, but I have found that I do not need that kind of relationship with another person. I prefer being on my own.

I have been told by a friend that my Picker is broken. And it made me laugh no end. But she is right. I cannot pick the right people to be with at all.

I have had three marriages and they all failed. I found that all my husbands wanted a slave, not a wife. While I don't mind sharing the chores, I don't like doing everything myself. If they had only made a cup of tea now and then, I would have been happy, but none of my husbands ever lifted a finger.

And as for keeping me company, I never found a partner who was even slightly interested in what I am interested in, so I might just as well have been alone even then.

I have also shared apartments with numerous people in my youth and have to say it was always a horrible experience. I remember all the flat mates in London with their little pats of butter with their name on them in the fridge, and all their clothes strewn about all over the place.

And then, when I owned my own house, a renter had a miscarriage in the bed, leaving the next day, and expecting me to replace the mattress.

I now belong to an art group, and a gym. Although there are people to pass the time of day with, I am definitely not good in a group setting. I make the effort to join in, but I don't feel comfortable at all. Often, I can't wait to get home.

I prefer a one-on-one situation where you can get to know the other person and they can get to know you. I have certain friends I see regularly for lunch and a chat. And I also write to about ten people online. That is all I need.

Over the years, many friends have moved away, or more likely I have moved away, and you lose touch. An email occasionally, a card at Christmas. That's what is left of so many friendships.

And as you get older, people die. You are really left alone then. If you are unlucky your life is spent going to other people's funerals. My brother, who is now 92, has no friends left.

I am certainly an introvert and spend my days writing at home. I used to be an extrovert when I was young, but something changed, and I can't tell you what it was. People change, that's all. Nothing stays the same. Life shapes you until you hardly recognize yourself sometimes.

I now prefer my own company. I am content with my not-so-perfect self and forgive myself for my mistakes.

What do I do when I feel like a piece of garbage with no redeeming qualities, and will I die alone because nobody cares enough about me?

You are in need of a great deal of love and a super big hug. But I know that is not forthcoming and nobody has hugged you in a very long time. That is how things are, and it is very sad indeed. We are all sentient beings, and we all deserve love.

I know all about this as it applies to me, too. I have lived alone now for the past twenty years and very rarely get a hug from anybody. You can't hold up a sign that says, "Please hug me." And, apart from that, if nobody loving is around, I can't think what else you can do if you are in need of a little loving.

The reason for this is that, when you don't have love, it is very tempting to think you must always get it from somebody else. From the outside. Surely, somebody out there should love us for who we are? It is only right, after all.

However, with this thought comes a painful knowing that love is not just going to happen, and we are not going to get that needed hug unless we ask for it. And who wants to ask for a hug.

So, as I see it, the only way to get some love is to give it to ourselves.

I decided this a long time ago and don't have any problem with love anymore. And if I need a hug, I wrap my arms around myself and give my body a well-needed squeeze. Funnily enough, when you learn to love yourself, your own hugs are just as satisfying as the ones other people give you. Try it and see.

This means we must learn to love ourselves in this lifetime, or we shall always be searching on the outside for the love we crave. It is a tall order, though, as it can take a very long time to love ourselves. But the sooner we practice, the better off we shall be.

In ideal circumstances, can you think of a loving relationship that knows no bounds? When I think of this question, I immediately think of a mother and baby as that kind of love is sacred. Most mothers love their babies unconditionally and give them all the hugs they need.

Picture that baby and allow yourself to feel like that baby in need of a good hug. Learn to love yourself in the way that the baby is loved.

If you are hungry, you need to be fed. If you are cold, you need to warm yourself up, and if you are tired, you need to sleep. These are the basic needs any baby has no matter what.

Now, think about what a good mother would do to love her baby no matter what.

It may take a bit of imagination at first, because we are not used to loving ourselves, but once you have the good mother in place, you will begin to see how easy it is to love yourself and to do things to make yourself happy. Never scold yourself, always be kind, give yourself whatever you need.

In other words, cherish the baby in you.

This is what I have done. I have a good mother who lives inside me. It has taken a long time, but it has been well worth it. I always tell myself good things and never cause myself harm. I say I am a kind, loving person and I truly believe I am. I think that is what a good mother would say to me. I also do things that are good for me and avoid things that upset me in any way.

Try it, and over time, you will begin to see changes in the way you treat yourself. And eventually you will feel the warmth of your love and won't need to get that big hug from anybody outside of you.

What happened to you by accident that changed your life for the better?

I am not sure what you mean by accident. Is it an accident that I met someone on Quora who has changed my life for the better? Maybe, maybe not.

Either way, I am very grateful to her because my life was very dull for many years. In fact, I never did anything at all to change my life in the twenty years prior to becoming her friend on Quora.

My husband died twenty-three years ago, and I lost hope for the future. I had no ambition to do anything, and passing my time was a big problem. The hours were long and boring. Looking back, I can't even remember what I did to pass the time except suffer the mood swings of bipolar disorder.

I know I must have done something else, but nothing that amounted to anything, and nothing I was proud of. I just thought I was biding my time until I died. And I wanted to die quite often because I was depressed most of the time. I was depressed with no ambition to even get well.

Then I met someone on Quora who changed the whole trajectory of my life. She said I should write a book. People had said that to me many times before because I have had a very interesting life, but I have never paid any attention to them. But when this person told me, I was very surprised because she is a renowned writer herself.

So, I mulled that over, then decided it would be worth a shot. I put everything else aside and wrote a book. It took me five months to complete and publish it on Amazon. And from that time on my life has changed for the better. The days aren't long and drawn out, and I have something I can hold in my hands and be proud of. Writing has been a life changing experience.

My only big regret is that I didn't start writing earlier. I waited until I was 73 to write anything worthwhile, now it is too late to make a career of it. I do my best but will never catch up with some writers who put out 20 books or more. There aren't enough years left.

The moral of this story is, don't wait around for that happy accident. If you have always wanted to do something but have put it off - go for it. It is never too late.

Nobody actually cares about me. What do I do now?

There is a major difference, as far as I can see, between caring for somebody and caring about them.

It is easy to care for somebody, doctors and nurses do it all the time, but caring about somebody takes love and commitment.

How many people can you count on one hand that you really care about? If you don't think people care about you, it is highly likely that you don't care about them.

Sometimes, people say they care about us, but have a funny way of showing it. If a person is harming us to the point of abuse, then it is pretty obvious that they do not care about us no matter what they say.

What do you do now?

It is a very sad situation when you feel this way. Many people have nobody who cares about them. Or they care about them conditionally.

I have been sick the past couple of days and the first day, a few people got in touch with me and offered help. Although they said they would call again, two more days have passed, and they have seemingly forgotten all about me.

I don't fret over this because I realize that it is life, and if you can get even one person to care about you, then you are luckier than most of us.

What causes some people to be happy alone while others need people around them all the time?

I have been alone for the past 23 years since my husband died of suicide. He was 16 years older than me and he was 70 when he died. Strangely enough, I never ever thought of him dying. It never occurred to me. Looking back, I realize that the age difference meant it was highly likely that he would die before me. I can't understand why it never occurred to me during our marriage.

But to expect him to die the way he did, from an overdose, would have been unthinkable. Indeed, I did not consider it at all. Suicide is always a shock to those left behind. He did leave a note, but it didn't explain why he decided to take his own life, so I shall never know what caused him to do that.

He was a depressive kind of man, meaning that he rarely found joy in life, but I didn't consider him depressed at the time of his death. I thought he was just being himself. Now, I can see that he must have been very depressed.

Suicide is a weird thing to face. You can't imagine what you could have done to cause such a breach of trust. No matter how much effort you have put into the marriage, it went unappreciated, and your spouse decided it wasn't enough. However, I never suffered from guilt, as I know I gave the marriage all I could for eighteen years. I did everything possible to ensure his happiness but, apparently, that was not enough.

I was very lonely for the first few years. I had no family in this country and only one brother left who lives in Australia. I had few friends because we had a very close marriage that didn't allow for other people in it. You could say we were co-dependent although I am not quite sure that is correct.

So, loneliness was a big problem for me for a very long period of time.

The strange thing is I did absolutely nothing for the next twenty years. The days, weeks and months passed very quickly, and I achieved nothing at all. When I look back now, twenty-two years later, I just can't imagine how I let life pass me by. I did try to join groups and keep busy but to no avail. Life just stopped.

I remember being very ill with bipolar disorder. This in itself took up many years of my time. You could say, I had no relief for a long time. I spent many months in hospital trying hard to get well. But despite all the treatment, my bipolar disorder was unrelenting.

Then I joined Quora and started writing on there. My whole world changed and slowly I became a different person. It took a lot of effort as I have written well over 5,000 answers, but gradually, over a period of 4 years, I became a person again.

It is not easy to describe the feelings of not being a person.

Most people would laugh at that as being a person is exactly who you are when you live in the world. Yet I could not become a person for so many years it became a natural state for me. If anything, I was like a little gray mouse who hid in corners away from people. I never made any noise and never asserted my independence.

But Quora changed all that, and I became the person I am today. Now I hardly have time to write on Quora because I am too busy with other things.

The way my life has changed is because I found things to do to keep my mind off being lonely and bored. I decided three years ago to write a book. It was a novel idea as I had never thought I had anything worth saying before. But again, Quora came to my rescue, and I wrote my book. Since then, it has been a good seller for me, and I know I have helped a lot of people, which gives me a great deal of pleasure.

I wrote a book about bipolar disorder called "How to Live with Bipolar" which I have suffered from all my life so had firsthand experience. I had no trouble writing it because I knew exactly how people felt who were inflicted by this cruel disease. Since then, I have written another book about bipolar. It is called "Bipolar 1 Disorder Rescue Plan" and is doing well for people who have bipolar 1 like myself.

Then I wrote my third book on bipolar disorder. It is called "37 Symptoms of Bipolar Depression." Many people have no idea what to do with all their symptoms of bipolar depression, so I wrote a workbook for them to fill in all the check lists and answer the questions that pertain to each symptom.

I also wrote a little book called "The Bipolar Guide" which is a condensed version of all my other books. In other words, it tells you what bipolar disorder is and how to cope with it.

I have also published a book on loneliness because I had a lot to say about that. It is called "A Practical Guide to Overcoming Loneliness," and is available on Amazon as well. I also wrote a book of poetry called "We Never Did

Mornings."

Now, I have branched out and am writing fiction. I have a 3-part series called Shards of Glass which is a new venture for me. I hope to write more fiction now because it is great fun.

So, I have told you this story to show you that loneliness does get better over time. It is painful to start with. Very painful indeed. But over time, things do improve, especially if you have something worthwhile to do with your life. Any distraction will do, but if it is a creative one, you will get enormous pleasure out of it and never feel lonely again.

I hope this has answered your question because I didn't expect to write so much about my life. But if it has helped just one person, I shall be happy.

Thank you very much for reading this book. I would really appreciate it if you could leave me a review on Amazon. Reviews help other people decide whether or not to read the book.

Thank you so much.

Sally.

My Books

NON FICTION

How to Live with Bipolar
Bipolar 1 Disorder Rescue Plan
37 Symptoms of Bipolar Depression
The Bipolar Guide
Life Lessons
A Practical Guide to Overcoming Loneliness

FICTION
(Pen name Dorothy Alter)

Shards of Glass Series
Shards of Glass
Fragments of the Past
Memories Lost in Time

SHORT STORIES
One Summer

POETRY
We Never Did Mornings

HUMOR
Funny Old Folk

List (c. Jan 2025)

About the author

Sally Alter is a prolific writer who has had bipolar disorder for over fifty years. She is also a Registered Nurse. After writing over 5,000 answers on the popular question and answer website Quora – 800 on bipolar alone – she realized her knowledge, compiled and condensed into books, could really help people.

Sally published her first book, *"How to Live with Bipolar"* at 73 and has gone on to publish three more books on bipolar - *"Bipolar 1 Disorder Rescue Plan,"* *"37 Symptoms of Bipolar Depression,"* and *"The Bipolar Guide."* Helping people and their families and friends through the stress and strain of bipolar has become her mission.

Sally is from London and now lives in Texas. She has traveled all over America in an RV and visited many European countries. When she is not writing, she can be found creating stunning oil paintings, doing colored pencil drawings, reading, completing jigsaw puzzles and spending time with Greta, her beloved cat.

Sally hopes her writing will fill in the gaps left by other bipolar disorder books to help people live more fulfilling lives.

For your **FREE** Bipolar Checklist visit https://sallyalter.com and subscribe to my newsletter

Or contact me here:

Facebook author page:
https://www.facebook.com/SallyAlterWriter/

Email address: mandala913@omniglobal.net

Freebie offer!

Get your freebie now. Go to my website and download my short story "One Summer" for **free**!

https://sallyalter.com/one-summer

www.ingramcontent.com/pod-product-compliance
Ingram Content Group UK Ltd.
Pitfield, Milton Keynes, MK11 3LW, UK
UKHW020746280225
455691UK00012B/472